ESSENTIAL LIBRARY OF THE
INFORMATION AGE

ONLINE IDENTITY

by Laura Perdew

CONTENT CONSULTANT
Dr. Sherali Zeadally
School of Information Science
University of Kentucky

Essential Library

An Imprint of Abdo Publishing | abdopublishing.com

abdopublishing.com

Published by Abdo Publishing, a division of ABDO, PO Box 398166, Minneapolis, Minnesota 55439. Copyright © 2017 by Abdo Consulting Group, Inc. International copyrights reserved in all countries. No part of this book may be reproduced in any form without written permission from the publisher. Essential Library™ is a trademark and logo of Abdo Publishing.

Printed in the United States of America, North Mankato, Minnesota
042016
092016

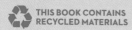

Cover Photo: Red Line Editorial
Interior Photos: Joe Raymond/AP Images, 5; Steve Debenport/iStockphoto, 7; Kelly Kline/Getty Images, 9; Apic/Getty Images, 11; Stephan Savoia/AP Images, 13; John Shearer/Invision for MTV/AP Images, 15; iStockphoto, 17, 21, 29, 49; Joel Carillet/iStockphoto, 19; Pichugin Dmitry/Shutterstock Images, 23; AP Images, 25; Alexey Boldin/Shutterstock Images, 26; Paul Sakuma/AP Images, 31; Waytao Shing/Getty Images for SXSW, 34; Monkey Business Images/iStockphoto, 37; Anatolii Babii/iStockphoto, 40; Google Plus/AP Images, 42; Jodi Jacobson/iStockphoto, 45; Rob Kim/Getty Images, 47; Pete Souza/White House, 52; Sean Gallup/Getty Images, 55; Lauren Elisabeth/Shutterstock Images, 57; Robyn Beck/AFP/Getty Images, 58; Jeremy Durkin/Rex Features/AP Images, 62; Dave Weaver/AP Images, 65; Gene J. Puskar/AP Images, 67; Evan Vucci/AP Images, 69; SolStock/iStockphoto, 71; David Duprey/AP Images, 72; Elizabeth Williams/AP Images, 75; David Goldman/AP Images, 76; John Badman/The Telegraph/AP Images, 79; Noriaki Sasaki/Yomiuri Shimbun/AP Images, 81; Hutton Supancic/WireImage/Getty Images, 83; Hussein Malla/AP Images, 85; Craig Ruttle/AP Images, 89; Miguel Villagran/Getty Images, 91; Josie Lepe/TNS/Newscom, 92; Rawpixel.com/Shutterstock Images, 94; DragonImages/iStockphoto, 97; Luba V. Nel/Shutterstock Images, 98

Editor: Arnold Ringstad
Series Designer: Craig Hinton

Publisher's Cataloging in Publication Data

Names: Perdew, Laura, author.
Title: Online identity / by Laura Perdew.
Description: Minneapolis, MN : Abdo Publishing, [2017] | Series: Essential library of the information age | Includes bibliographical references and index.
Identifiers: LCCN 2015960311 | ISBN 9781680782875 (lib. bdg.) | ISBN 9781680774764 (ebook)
Subjects: LCSH: Online identities--Juvenile literature. | Internet safety measures --Juvenile literature. | Internet--Juvenile literature.
Classification: DDC 302.23--dc23
LC record available at http://lccn.loc.gov/2015960311

CONTENTS

CHAPTER 1

IDENTITY

Coming out of high school, Manti Te'o was one of the top football players in the United States, and he had his pick of colleges. He signed with the University of Notre Dame, became a team leader, and went on to earn All-American honors. In 2009, Te'o met a woman online and began a committed relationship with her. Although they never met in person, Te'o and Lennay Kekua spoke on the phone and communicated regularly. Kekua even exchanged text messages with Te'o's parents.

Then, tragically, she was diagnosed with leukemia. She died in September 2012, around the same time Te'o's grandmother died. Twice heartbroken, Te'o poured his grief into his play on the field. In public statements following big wins over rival schools, Te'o said he believed these two important women in his life were with him during the games. It was a media sensation. But in December, reporters began to question whether Kekua had really died, or if she had even existed at all, despite her believable online identity. The frenzy that followed ultimately revealed Te'o was the victim of a cruel hoax, leaving him humiliated and confused about Kekua's true identity.

Football player Manti Te'o found himself at the center of an online identity controversy in 2012.

CATFISHING

Online relationships have become more common in the early 2000s. In many cases, the people involved do not meet in person for a long time. In Manti Te'o's case, he believed he was in an authentic relationship with Lennay Kekua. As it turned out, someone had created a false online identity in order to fool Te'o into a relationship with someone who did not exist. Te'o was the victim of a practice called *catfishing*, or tricking someone into forming an online relationship with a nonexistent person. The term comes from the 2010 documentary *Catfish*, in which a man begins an online romantic relationship with a woman and then discovers she never existed.

WHAT IS IDENTITY?

Identity is the sum of a complex set of values and characteristics that guides people's actions throughout their lives. Many things, including family, religion, community, race, gender, and education, influence these values and beliefs. Characteristics can include both personality traits, such as being positive or cynical, and physical traits, such as skills at sports or music. All of these elements are interconnected. Together they become the identity a person presents to the world.

People present different parts of their identities in different contexts. A teenager may present one side of himself at the skate park after school, but another when visiting his grandmother. Further, one's identity is never stable. It is always changing as a result of new experiences, relationships, and social and cultural influences.

Identity formation is especially complex in adolescence, as teens experiment with different identities to find a true sense

The context of a school lunch with peers is likely to bring out different sides of a person's identity than he or she might show in other situations and places.

of who they are. They may struggle to fit in and to discover their individuality. During this process, teens may try on different roles and explore different sets of values.

Identities can also be created out of nothing. This is especially easy online. In Lennay Kekua's case, she did not have a real-world identity. The photo for her online profile was an image of someone else, and the hoaxer made up the details of her online identity. The woman Te'o spoke with on the phone was a real person pretending to be Kekua.

TE'O: SCAMMED, OR SCAMMER?

Following news stories about Manti Te'o's girlfriend, speculation arose about Te'o's possible involvement in the scam because of inconsistencies in the story. Te'o's father reported Te'o had met the woman in person, though it appeared this did not really happen. Te'o admitted he tailored his stories to make people think they had met.

Lennay Kekua reportedly died in September 2012, but in early December Te'o reportedly got a call from the woman posing as Kekua saying she was not actually dead. Despite this, Te'o continued to talk about his girlfriend, and her death, publicly for some time, saying he was not convinced Kekua was still alive. Ultimately, he revealed to his Notre Dame coaching staff what had occurred, and a private investigator was hired. Some people believed Te'o was in on the scam for personal gain and publicity. But Te'o maintained his innocence even as speculation swirled around him, stating that he was the "victim of what was apparently someone's sick joke and constant lies."[1] Eventually, investigative reporters uncovered the truth. An old friend of Te'o's had carried out the hoax. It was unclear why he had done it.

Te'o received extensive media attention in the wake of the revelations about his online relationship.

THE INTERNET

The Internet was created by engineers, programmers, scholars, and researchers who wanted to connect computers in order to communicate and share information. As early as the 1930s, Belgian information expert Paul Otlet envisioned a network of telephone wires and radio waves that would allow people to do just that. The roots of today's Internet, however, did not take hold until the 1960s. During this decade, the Department of Defense's Advanced Research Projects Agency in the United States began a computer network project designed to share information. The agency soon discovered sending a whole message via phone lines was too slow, so it created a system that broke messages into smaller pieces encoded with the messages' intended destination. When these pieces, called *packets*, reached their destination, they were pieced back together and the whole message was delivered. The first computer-to-computer communication was

CYBERPSYCHOLOGY

People are having increasing numbers of experiences and relationships in the virtual world. A new branch of psychology has emerged: cyberpsychology. Traditional psychology examines how the human mind functions and how this functioning affects behavior. The emerging field of cyberpsychology focuses on the intersection of technology and the human experience. It investigates how people behave in the virtual world. Cyberpsychologists also study the impact social media, mobile devices, online games, and other technologies have on individuals.

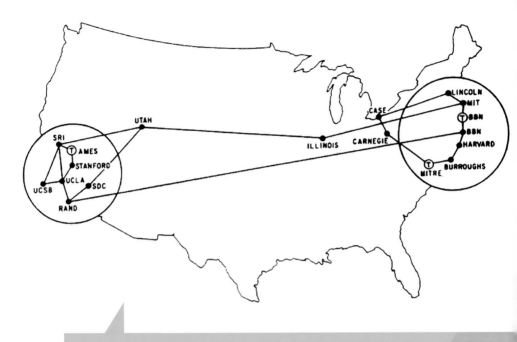

By 1972, an early form of the Internet connected only a few
research facilities in the United States.

sent on October 29, 1969. The system crashed partway through the
transmission. Still, the foundation had been laid.

As personal computer technology advanced in the 1970s
and 1980s, people began to create their own networks. However,
most were limited to communicating within a single network.
Researchers developed a system called Transmission Control
Protocol and Internet Protocol (TCP/IP) that at last allowed
computers on different networks to talk to each other. On
January 1, 1983, TCP/IP became the universal language that
connected all networks. A computer connected to this vast
network of networks, known as the Internet, could communicate
and share information with any other connected computer on
the planet.

As children grow, one part of identity they must explore in order to find a true sense of who they are is their gender. Gender identity has to do with identifying with one gender or another, and acting according to cultural expectations of that gender. Some people are born as biologically male or female but identify more closely with another gender. They may feel uncomfortable with the gender their body dictates. This is known as gender dysphoria. In the real world, youth struggling with gender dysphoria often experience isolation, bullying, and depression. The virtual world, however, can provide them with a safe place to explore their identity.

Using the early version of the Internet required an understanding of the routes that connected computers in order to access or share information. Then in 1989, researcher Tim Berners-Lee conceptualized the idea of linking ideas. Under this system, users could easily jump between linked ideas instead of moving between computers. The result of Berners-Lee's work was the World Wide Web, which is accessed via the Internet. The concept of the web was introduced to the public in 1990. Berners-Lee also wrote the first web browser, establishing many of the browser conventions still used today. Along with search engines, browsers make it easy for users to search the web and view information there.

The Internet and the web have created a whole other world. This other world, sometimes known as cyberspace, has no physical location or boundaries. It is constructed entirely through communication networks. People who participate in

In 1994, Berners-Lee founded the World Wide Web Consortium, a group that develops standards for the web.

the virtual world can be a part of communities and experiences separate from the real world. The identities people present to others in this world are influenced by both real and virtual interactions and experiences.

IDENTITY MEETS THE INTERNET

In the virtual world, people construct their online identities in much the same way as in the real world. The difference is that the virtual world has fewer limits. In the real world, there are physical restrictions on where one can go, and most interactions are face-to-face. But on the Internet, people can talk with just about anyone they want. Users can join communities, build online relationships, and access seemingly limitless amounts of entertainment and information. They may feel the freedom to define themselves in any way they want, knowing they are unlikely to encounter people they meet online in the physical world.

PET PROFILES: GRUMPY CAT

In the virtual world, even a cat can have an online identity. Grumpy Cat became a virtual sensation after her owner posted photos of her on the Internet in 2012. Her perpetually grumpy-looking face, caused in part by her feline dwarfism, caught people's attention, and her popularity continued to increase. Grumpy Cat has not only her own website, but also a Facebook page, a Twitter account, Instagram photos, and YouTube videos.

Pet owners can even create online identities for their animals. Fans took selfies with one of these pets, Grumpy Cat, at an event in 2014.

Online identities have become major parts of everyday life. Their emergence has brought about new controversies and problems. Social networks, dating websites, online games, and many online activities are closely linked with these new identities. Experts, policymakers, and everyday people are working to learn what the idea of modern identity means for privacy, crime, relationships, and other aspects of life in the information age. The connection between online and offline identities is one of the defining elements of today's digital world.

CHAPTER 2

IDENTITY AND SOCIAL INTERACTION

In some cultures, a person's identity is almost entirely defined by membership in that culture. There is little notion of individual identity, except for the roles a person plays in the culture. Men, for example, may be responsible for leadership and providing food, while women's identities may be tied to more domestic tasks. Elders may be looked to for wisdom and guidance. Still, people's idea of the self is tied to the collective clan, tribe, band, family, or group. In fact, the languages used in such cultures sometimes even lack the word *I*, and people instead use the word *we*.

As Western society developed and modernized, the notion of individual identity emerged. The Middle Ages show evidence of this. During this time, people wrote a growing number of autobiographies and commissioned more family and individual portraits. People used individual chairs rather than communal benches, and more homes had private rooms. This evidence suggests people began to define themselves less by group identity and became more self-aware of their individual identities.

Devices such as smartphones and selfie sticks have forever changed the way people create and share their individual identities.

The increase in the complexity of societies also made it more difficult for large groups to form a common identity. People lived farther apart and became less connected to more distant neighbors. When individuals live in a large, spread-out city, the fact that they all live in the city may be the only thing that binds them together.

Even in today's Western world, physical, social, and geographic factors are still important to people's individual identities. And up until the early 2000s, life was mostly private, limited to interactions with family, neighbors, coworkers, and friends. It was recorded only through public records, stories, and photographs taken with film. Associating with groups involved real-world interactions or possessions. A fan of a football team would buy and wear that team's jersey. A religious believer would go to church services. Teenagers might meet to hang out at the mall. Even in these cases, the identity one presented to the world generally reached a relatively small, private audience.

IDENTITY IN A VIRTUAL WORLD

In the age of the Internet, a person's identity reaches a global audience. Individuals can broadcast ideas, opinions, photos, interests, and videos across the world for anyone to see, promoting their sense of who they are. One of the most powerful aspects of

> 66 When I say, 'The Internet changes everything,' I really mean everything. 99 [1]
> —Larry Ellison, CEO of software company Oracle, 1999

Even in the age of social networking, church services and other community gatherings remain important venues where people can express their identities.

THE RIGHT TO BE FORGOTTEN

Online information has the potential to remain accessible forever. That includes one's online identity. Businesses, government organizations, and even other individuals can monitor and collect data on people via their social media use, web search history, photos, online purchases, posts, and more. There is little the individual can do about it. As a result, there is a growing coalition of people fighting for the right to be forgotten. The initiative began in Europe. The European Commission has put a privacy measure in place that lets Internet users decide for themselves what aspects of their personal data stay online. The measure is described as "the right of any individual to see himself or herself represented in a way that is not inconsistent with his/her current personal and social identity."[2] It gives the individual the right to control his or her online identity.

The debate has reached the United States as more people call for the same rights and controls. By 2016, some states had enacted laws with varying degrees of protections, but there were no federal laws granting citizens the right to be forgotten.

this online identity is that it can be carefully crafted to represent the person someone aspires to be. In the real world, one cannot easily conceal gender, race, age, ethnicity, or even personality, but in the virtual world the construction of identity is up to the individual.

A group of British scientists published a report in 2013 that proposed the Internet is redefining identity. Traditional elements of one's identity, such as religion, ethnicity, or age, are less significant online. On the Internet, people can find their place in the world without ever leaving town. They can more easily connect with like-minded individuals in the virtual world. In other words, the Internet is changing not just identity, but the idea of community.

People who use wheelchairs or who have other physical limitations can experience a lower risk of prejudiced treatment online than they might in the offline world.

Additionally, in the virtual world people are able to escape preconceptions or stereotypes based on their physical status. For instance, a person in a wheelchair has physical limitations in the real world; people he or she meets may have preconceived notions about what he or she can or cannot do. But in the virtual world, it is possible to remove this potential for prejudice. People can socialize with each other on a more level playing field. The same is true for those who may be shy, awkward, or self-conscious about their appearance. The freedom of their online identities may let them socialize more comfortably. Some people feel as though their online identities enable them to express their true selves for the first time.

SOCIALIZING AND COMMUNICATION

Just as the concept of individual identity changed as society became more complex, so have the ways in which people socialize. Even in prehistoric times, individuals posted information, in the form of cave paintings, petroglyphs, and pictographs, for their fellow members of society to see. As cultures became larger and more complex, areas such as Roman city halls and forums became the designated places for socializing.

There were forms of rapid communication, too. Peoples across the globe, including the Incas and Greeks, sent important information via relay runners. These runners formed a simple network, passing messages from one runner to the next until they reached the

EARLY 1900s SOCIAL NETWORKING

Before online social networks, people did their networking in person. Sometimes this was done at a cracker barrel—a real barrel from which crackers used to be served in local general stores in the late 1800s and early 1900s. These general stores, which sold a variety of items, including food and hardware, were gathering places in areas where people typically went to town only rarely. Merchants sought to make their stores attractive places to spend time, so they put out barrels of crackers for patrons to snack on while in the store.

Cave paintings were one way in which prehistoric people could share information with their social networks.

intended audience. Written messages had to be carefully copied by hand, a labor-intensive process. After the invention of the printing press, people could get their news and information from printed materials distributed to wide audiences. Eventually they used postal services, telegraphs, telephones, and radios to spread messages to large numbers of people.

Social networking before the Internet was done mostly face-to-face or over the phone. These interactions took place in business meetings, in neighborhoods, through schools, and at social clubs, and they happened in real time. These experiences both reflected individual identities and helped shape them. The virtual world is different: interactions take place in virtual communities.

> "The fantastic advances in the field of electronic communication constitute a great danger to the privacy of the individual." [3]
>
> —Chief Justice Earl Warren, 1963

Online social networks emerged at the same time the Internet developed. One of the first was the Bulletin Board System (BBS). The BBS allowed users to share information on a variety of subjects and quickly gained popularity in the 1980s and 1990s. Other networks that gained popularity beginning in the 1980s were CompuServe and America Online, both of which offered interaction in discussion forums and member communities, as well as the ability to send e-mails.

By the mid-1990s Yahoo was gaining popularity, followed at the beginning of the new millennium by Friendster, MySpace, and then Facebook and Twitter. Registered users on these sites

By 1980, users of CompuServe could access news headlines on their personal computers over the Internet.

CompuServe   Page 68
        THE COLUMBUS DISPATCH
1 Top News Briefs
2 US/World News
3 Local/Ohio News
4 Political Campaigns
5 Sports
6 Business
7 Opinion/Editorial
8 Leisure/Entertainment

Last menu page. Key digit
or M for previous menu.   !

The Columbus Dispatch

OHIO'S GREATEST HOME NEWSPAPER
Columbus, Ohio 43216, Wednesday, July 9, 1980

HOME
FINAL

15 Cents

7 Die As Crowds Await Papal Visit

HISTORY OF FACEBOOK

Facebook is older than most people know. The original facebook began at Harvard University in the 1970s. This physical book, which was distributed on campus, included the names, photos, and addresses of each class of students. The directory of photos became a central part of students' social lives, and some even admitted to looking for potential dates in the printed facebook. Other students simply used it to get to know classmates' names or to try to see what people were like. When Harvard student Mark Zuckerberg launched his social networking site in 2004, he borrowed the term *facebook*. He quickly had thousands of users signed up and creating profiles. It was so well received that the network soon extended to other colleges, then high schools, and then the general public. By 2016, Facebook remained one of the largest and most successful social networking sites in the world.

can connect to friends both old and new, creating an online community of people to interact with. Other sites, such as LinkedIn, focus on creating professional and business networks. Still others focus on niche topics, including forums for support groups, politics, dating, health, music, art, and more. Mobile technology has furthered bolstered the popularity of social networking sites, allowing people to stay connected and interact almost constantly. Mobile devices also gave rise to photo- and video-sharing applications such as Snapchat and Instagram. Today, many people use numerous platforms to network. This allows them to develop a comprehensive online identity.

More than 1.5 billion people had created a profile on Facebook by 2016.

CHAPTER 3

THE SECOND SELF

People may have several overlapping identities. An individual teenager can be a friend, a brother, a son, a babysitter, a gamer, and many other things. Some of these are personal preferences. But some aspects of identity are grounded in the reality of the physical world. There is nothing people can do to change their age or ethnicity. People are also constrained by their actual physical locations and by social expectations in creating their real-life identities. But in the 2000s, the Internet made it possible to create online identities not limited by these factors.

IDENTITY CONSTRUCTION

When creating an online identity, a person begins with a nearly blank slate. He or she begins with creating an online profile, which includes choosing a screen name and an e-mail address. From there, building the profile involves questions that can include general information about age, birthday, and location, as well as more personal questions about interests, fears, and dislikes. Each answer becomes a piece of a virtual identity. This carefully constructed identity allows individuals to present the very best

Creating an online identity can be a freeing experience for people who wish to escape the limitations of their offline lives.

parts of themselves to the world, while omitting the parts they do not like.

One major component of an online profile is the profile picture. Users must decide what kind of profile picture to use. This choice can communicate information about them and helps shape their online identity. Perhaps the photo is of the person on a football field. Maybe it shows them wearing a fancy dress. It may show off their elaborate makeup, or it may show them with messy hair and wearing pajamas soon after waking up. Some people may choose photos with friends to show off their social side, or to demonstrate their friendship with certain people. Still others use an avatar, a fictional representation of themselves.

People also build their online identities by posting thoughts, opinions, and ideas on their own websites, social media profiles, blogs, or Twitter accounts. Visiting and

BOYS VERSUS GIRLS

Technology and social media are integral to the social lives of teens in the digital age. However, a study released in 2015 revealed differences in how boys and girls use technology to socialize. Girls, for example, tend to use social media sites such as Facebook or Instagram much more frequently than boys. Boys tend to turn more to video games as a means of socializing. This holds true both for making new friends and for keeping up with existing friends. Girls are also much more likely to unfriend or block someone on social media after a friendship ends. Text messaging remains the most popular way for both boys and girls to use technology to communicate, but girls do so with much greater frequency than boys.

Facebook creator Mark Zuckerberg introduced changes to
Facebook's profile pages in 2011.

responding to material in other parts of the virtual world also
builds identity. For example, clicking the "like" button on Facebook
or Twitter can communicate a person's interests. In addition,
individuals can share photos, news articles, and other online
content with others through social media, further building their
online identities.

For teens, a critical aspect of identity formation is establishing
an identity that is separate from their families. The Internet allows

LIKES

How many "likes" a user gets on social media has turned into a type of social currency. Marketers have realized the power of the like. In the past, companies marketed products to potential consumers through placement in specific magazines, newspapers, television shows, and radio stations. Marketers created the ad, and consumers bought the product. The virtual world has changed that, and consumers are now engaging with products online. Businesses are happy to amass likes for their products. They collect data about online interactions, such as likes, retweets, and shares, to give them a better sense of who their customers are. They use this information to more precisely target future advertising.

them to do just that, providing a platform on which to explore new identities. This space is vastly different from the real world. Individuals are free to roam wherever they like at any hour of the day or night—there is no need for driving a car, having to ask permission to leave the house, or worrying about a curfew. Teenagers only a few decades ago could only dream about such independence.

DIGIPHRENIA

As the virtual world becomes a more pervasive aspect of life in the 2000s, larger numbers of people are creating multiple online identities. Some experts are concerned about the effects of trying to exist in more than one place at the same time. Media theory and digital economics scholar Douglas Rushkoff calls this phenomenon digiphrenia, based on the Latin word *phrenia*, or disordered thinking. This divided attention also sacrifices a person's connections to the real world. Rushkoff believes the digital era results in a sense of timelessness; people no longer live by the cycles of the sun, instead living constantly in the present. This leaves their online identities anchored by snapshots of what's current.

Others do not see a problem. Even in the real world, people have multiple identities that may or may not overlap. To this way of thinking, one's online identity is merely an extension of the real self. The Internet gives people the freedom to explore identity without limitations or prejudices. Sherry Turkle, professor of the social studies of science and technology at the Massachusetts Institute of Technology, maintains, "No one aspect can be claimed as the absolute, true self."[1] She believes that by exploring identity in the virtual world, people are given the opportunity to get to know their "inner diversity."[2] The key, according to Turkle, is coming to terms with all parts of one's self and being able to combine these parts into a single, whole identity.

REBECCA BLACK

Like so many other teens, aspiring singer Rebecca Black had an online presence. Her parents paid a music production company to film a music video for her, and in 2011 Black's video was uploaded to YouTube. Within three weeks, the video of her singing the song "Friday" had received more than 38 million hits, putting Black squarely in the limelight. Her instant online fame also made her a target for hatred, trolling, and cyberbullying by those critical of the song and its lyrics. Initially, Rebecca was upset by the hateful comments. Her mother even suggested they take down the video, but Rebecca said, "No, it's my right to have my video up there. Why should I have to take my video down?"[3] Black even used the money she made from "Friday" to fund another song and video.

Rushkoff gives a presentation about the effects of the Internet on daily life at the South by Southwest festival in Austin, Texas, in 2013.

UNINTENTIONAL IDENTITIES

One part of online identity of which many people are unaware is that much of their identity is created for them, not by them. While they may feel in control of their social media profiles, blog posts, and shared personal information, they may not consider other parts of their online identity. For example, while social media posts are an obvious part of online identity, things such as product reviews on Amazon.com and restaurant criticisms on Yelp help build identity too.

Sometimes online identity is completely out of a person's control. Friends or family members may post photos or comments about someone on their own social media pages, indirectly constructing that person's online identity. A photo taken in a goofy, unguarded moment with friends may be entirely inappropriate when viewed by a parent, teacher, or pastor. A person may also appear online on the website of a school or organization. Many public records are available online, including arrest records and police booking photos. All of these things can add up to a significant online presence, even if a person tries to avoid revealing personal information online.

EXPRESSING OFFLINE IDENTITY

Throughout history, people have found ways to demonstrate their identity to others. They have used body ornamentation as a means of expressing kinship and belonging, through body painting, piercings, tattoos, headdresses, clothing, veils, uniforms, hairstyles, and makeup. Flags and crests are also used to show familial or national identity. Today people express their offline identities in much the same ways. They also use newer tools to show off their identities, such as bumper stickers, ball caps, banners, and logos.

CHAPTER 4

WHO IS LOOKING?

When hanging out with friends in the school cafeteria at lunchtime, students can see clearly who is around. They present certain sides of themselves that likely differ from the sides they present with the debate club after school, at the family dinner table, and at a grandmother's house. If a teacher or other adult walks by, conversations may pause until the coast is clear. This is because where one is, and who else is present, contribute to the way people behave and the identity they present. People consider both audience and context when presenting themselves in the real world. The difficulty in the virtual world is that the audience is invisible and there is little consistent context.

AUDIENCE

Managing one's online identity becomes complicated without direct knowledge of context or audience. Invited friends and family follow each other online. But who else is looking? The safe answer is, just about everyone. Teachers can potentially see what their students are posting online. And college admissions offices can investigate applicants' online presences. Employers, enemies,

With many modern forms of communication, including texting and social media posting, there's no guarantee that only the intended recipient is reading messages.

bullies, banks, organizations, law enforcement, cybercriminals, or someone with a crush all might search for individuals online and easily find who they are looking for. Many of the people in this audience are strangers to the individual and most are harmless. But there are also identity thieves, scammers, catfishers, and predators, all lurking around the Internet looking for victims.

In addition, even with social media privacy settings in place or having only a small number of followers, a person's audience is often much larger than he or she imagines it to be. Communication thought to be private can end up being quite public. Such was the case with 30-year-old Justine Sacco. During a layover on a long international flight, she tweeted sarcastic jokes about travel to her 170 followers. Some of her barbs were directed toward passengers with foul body odor or bad teeth. Just before getting on the plane for the last leg of travel to South Africa,

ONLINE DATING

As of 2015, more than 40 million people had tried using online dating services.[1] As with creating other online identities, using these websites begins with creating a profile. While many experience anxiety about building this persona, scientists have actually figured out what works best. For example, one of the hardest parts of the profile may be choosing a photo. Experts found that people responded best to photos with a genuine smile, and to those where the individual is with others having fun. They found that people also responded well to profiles where the individual did not come across as self-centered, where the messages were meaningful and positive, and where there were no grammatical or spelling errors.

she tweeted, "Going to Africa. Hope I don't get AIDS. Just kidding. I'm white!"[2]

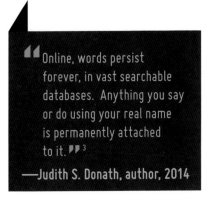

"Online, words persist forever, in vast searchable databases. Anything you say or do using your real name is permanently attached to it."[3]

—Judith S. Donath, author, 2014

By the time Sacco landed 11 hours later, her tweet had received major attention. Twitter had exploded with outrage about her racist and highly insensitive comment, and Sacco herself was horrified. In the aftermath, Sacco's family in South Africa was disgraced, hotel workers where Sacco was booked threatened to go on strike if she showed up, angry tweets continued, her story became a media sensation, and she lost her job. What had been intended to be a jab at the bubble of privilege in which she lived ended up ruining her life because Sacco's audience was not just 170 people. Retweeted, her message reached a global audience that was unaware of the context in which the joke was intended.

CONTEXT

In the real world, it is easy to understand the context in which interactions take place, such as a kitchen, a gym, or a mall. In the virtual world, some individuals believe they are keeping their identities separate depending on the virtual context, just as they would in the real world. But given the nature of the Internet, this is not always possible. Online, people's worlds collide, intersect, and interact in ways that are difficult to anticipate or see because there are no physical constraints.

This happened to a young African-American ninth grader living in Washington, DC, who regularly posted to Facebook. He described his sister and cousins as "ghetto," but his friends were high-achieving kids from the magnet school he attended. He was able to keep these two aspects of his life separate in the real world, but on Facebook they collided. The boy wanted to talk to his school friends one way and his family and neighborhood friends another, but on Facebook people from both parts of his life were able to see and criticize his posts. This led to frustration on his part. When his interactions occurred face-to-face, the boy did not have to monitor or curb what he said because the context was clear.

COCA-COLA'S SOCIAL MEDIA SUCCESS

Coca-Cola has worldwide recognition. In order to market Coke to such a broad audience, the company keeps a unified brand message while simultaneously targeting certain audiences in different regions or countries. It also uses social media such as Twitter, where it has more than 3 million followers.[4] Coca-Cola takes advantage of these users by Tweeting dozens of times a day. It also engages users by inviting them to create and share Coca-Cola–related content, essentially having the public promote its products online. The company also uses Tumblr, Instagram, videos, and Facebook. The key to Coca-Cola's success lies in the fact that it carefully monitors its social media presence and tailors content to what consumers want.

Many Twitter users have discovered their messages can travel much more widely than originally intended.

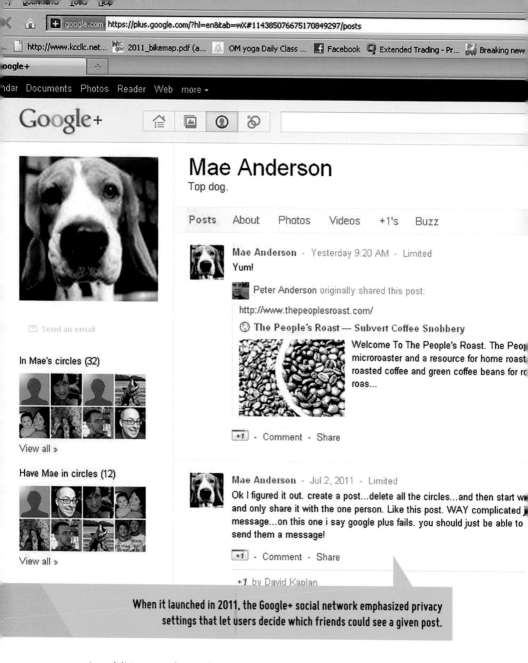

When it launched in 2011, the Google+ social network emphasized privacy settings that let users decide which friends could see a given post.

In addition to physical spaces, context also refers to time. In the real world, much is forgotten or fades out of memory over time. An embarrassing fall in the school hallway that sends books flying might be part of conversation for a day or a week, but then it will likely be forgotten. Rumors generally fade out, too. On the other hand, the virtual world preserves things. While online posts or photos may be years old, people can still see them. So even if the information about one's identity is outdated, it is still available online for a college admissions officer or prospective employer to discover. Unflattering photos or angry rants on social media may have been posted long ago, but to anyone who finds them they exist in the present.

Invisible audiences and collapsed context make creating and managing an online personality even more challenging than identity formation in the real world. These features of online identities have changed the way people communicate and socialize.

CHAPTER 5

REDEFINING RELATIONSHIPS

The Internet has changed the way people interact and communicate with one another. There is debate, however, over whether this is a good thing. Some believe virtual communication is disconnecting people in the real world, while others argue it enhances relationships. Many teens fall into the latter category. They experience the benefits of social media, which gives them places to share their opinions, hang out, participate, and socialize in ways never experienced by past generations.

DISCONNECTED?

Despite this increased connectedness, some worry individuals are becoming ever more disconnected, focused on their devices instead of on face-to-face relationships. Sherry Turkle argues that instead of connecting people, technology is isolating them. In her work, Turkle has discovered more and more people shy away from real conversations in favor of a text, e-mail, or some other short digital message. Her research revealed part of people's hesitation with real-time conversations is that it is more difficult to control

Turkle argues overuse of digital technology can lead to reduced social interaction in the real world.

the identity they present. Online conversations, on the other hand, give individuals the time to present the self they want to be.

Turkle also suggests that with digital communications people are only partially participating in a conversation at any one time, never devoting their full attention to it. This phenomenon often happens in conversations with friends after school. A group might gather to walk home together, to get coffee, or maybe to study. During that conversation it is not uncommon for someone to pull out a phone and shift out of the real world and into a virtual one. This leads to disconnection.

> "Human relationships are rich and they're messy and they're demanding. And we clean them up with technology."[1]
>
> —Sherry Turkle, digital media expert, February 2012

In the modern world, where people are simultaneously connected to the real and virtual world, real-world conversations can leave individuals feeling like no one is listening because attentions are divided. Thus, to be heard, people may develop their online personas to find an audience of willing listeners. Technology makes possible a form of communication that does not carry the demands of real-time conversations.

Some studies show overuse of social media can lead to depression, anxiety, and other psychological disorders. Larry D. Rosen, professor of psychology at California State University,

Professor Sherry Turkle studies how technology and online social networks can affect people's relationships.

presented the findings of his psychological research in a talk titled "Poke Me: How Social Networks Can Both Help and Harm Our Kids." One of his key findings is that teens who use Facebook excessively tend to have antisocial behaviors, may be in danger of health problems related to Internet addiction, and are distracted from schoolwork, sometimes resulting in lower grades.

POSITIVE EFFECTS

Despite the research, and the worry of well-meaning parents, teens themselves report the digital world allows them to feel more connected to their real-world friends and even make new friends. In addition, teens say social media helps them better support friends in times of need.

For some teens, the Internet is liberating in a way they have never before been able to experience. One teen explained that

Social media gives people the opportunity to connect with friends regardless of where they are physically.

SLACKTIVISM

Critics of online activism say it is a slacker's way of participating without getting off the couch, describing it as *slacktivism*. For instance, some people have tinted their profile pictures online in solidarity with particular causes. But some online campaigns can bring about real-world results. Following the earthquake in Haiti in 2010, for example, online activism spurred more than $30 million in fund-raising in a few months.[4]

oftentimes getting together with friends in the real world was difficult. She said, "If you don't have the option [of getting together in person], then you can just go online."[3] Given constraints of location, transportation, homework, house rules, and curfews, teens are often limited in the time they can spend with friends face-to-face. So instead of sneaking out of the house, kids can now sneak onto social media between math problems to hang out with friends, providing them with the opportunity to relax and socialize on their own terms.

In contrast to Turkle's claims, studies have found that all of this virtual socializing has actually led to an increase in empathy in teens. When teens learn friends are facing difficulties, they are able to give emotional support immediately. Learning the art of empathizing in the virtual world, according to Rosen, can also help teens learn how to empathize in the real world. He also asserts that creating an online identity and managing it successfully can be useful for teens who are naturally shy or introverted. The virtual world gives them the chance to practice socializing in a relatively risk-free environment.

Having an online identity also gives individuals, including teens, a voice. They gain the opportunity to participate in public life both in their own community and globally. For teens, being involved in social or political issues in the real world can be daunting or simply not feasible. Some report their real-world friends do not share their concerns with social issues around the world. Their online activism enables them to connect with other people thinking about the same issues. One college student reported that her circle of real-world friends was not much interested in global women's issues, nor did she think of herself as an activist. But then she found herself drawn to posts and links on social media sites and has become increasingly active in order to create change. About using the virtual world to create

ONLINE ACTIVISM MAKES A DIFFERENCE

The online organization DoSomething.org is designed for young people who want to make a difference in the world. The organization boasts more than five million members from 130 countries.[5] Its campaigns aim to make tangible, real-world changes for the better. On the site, individuals can choose from a variety of campaigns in which to take part. The campaigns include connecting with seniors to teach them about technology, making friends aware of products tested on animals, and organizing a trash scavenger hunt to clean up parks. Many of the initiatives are simple, but with many people participating, they can create real change.

Barack Obama was the first president in history to have an online identity. Recognizing the platform for reaching the American public had changed dramatically since his predecessor took office, Obama turned to social media even before he was elected. Once in the White House, he put together a team of 14 staff members in the newly created White House Office of Digital Strategy.[7] Obama leveraged social media not only to reach wide audiences, but also to target groups disconnected from mainstream politics. In addition, Obama understood the participatory nature of today's online culture and invited the public to "engage and connect" on a White House website.[8] The site is a social hub for all things politics, and it encourages online users to take part in discussions, learn about initiatives, ask questions, send e-mails, and submit feedback.

real-world change, one blogger said, "We're organizing, we're creating, we're signal-boosting, we're creating awareness. We're changing the world."[6] People, teens included, use their online identities to spread the word about issues that matter to them, and they believe it is a powerful way to spread a message to a large audience quickly.

> " A lot of physical protests and movements are very localized, but online there are no limits to who can engage with you. "[9]
>
> —Melissa, teen online activist, 2014

President Obama was the first president to heavily leverage smartphones and social media in his campaigns and during his time in office.

CHAPTER 6

THE ALTER EGO IN ACTION

The word *avatar* has become closely associated with online activities, including gaming. But it has its origins in Hinduism, a religion whose history goes back thousands of years. It refers to the human form of gods on earth. When computer gaming gained popularity in the 1990s, the word took on a new meaning. Today an avatar is a figure people choose to represent themselves, either in a game or online generally. Some people see the use of an avatar in online games as the ultimate form of an independent online identity. As people spend more time in virtual worlds, experts are weighing what avatars mean for their overall well-being and real-world identities.

CREATING AN AVATAR

Avatars are one of the most clearly visible ways people build their online identities. The use of avatars, especially in gaming, gives people a significant measure of control over the identities they present to the online world. This is remarkably similar to the ways in which people attempt to manipulate their appearance in the real world, changing hairstyle, clothing, and makeup. In the

In online games such as *World of Warcraft*, users may spend hundreds of hours role playing as their avatars.

real world, there are limits to how much one can change one's appearance. In the virtual world, though, these limits are gone.

While there has been a trend toward avatars that represent a person's real-world self, some people still choose avatars that allow them to escape the limitations of their own bodies or the preconceived notions people have of them in the real world. Others believe avatars empower them to find their true identity without the confines of real-world limits. Consider the case of Jason Rowe, a young man with significant physical disabilities. As a result of muscular dystrophy, he has little muscle control over his body, and he uses a ventilator to breathe. However, Rowe does have some control over his thumbs, so he can play online games. The avatar he has chosen for himself is a physical opposite of his real-world self. It is a steel-plated, robotic figure that can speed around on bikes, battle monsters, and socialize with friends. Being online lets Rowe interact with people and be treated equally, without any prejudices dictated

> " In the traditional community, we search through our pool of neighbours and professional colleagues, of acquaintances and acquaintances of acquaintances, in order to find people who share our values and interests. . . . In a virtual community we can go directly to the place where our favourite subjects are being discussed, then get acquainted with people who share our passions or who use words in a way we find attractive. Your chances of making friends are magnified by orders of magnitude over the old methods of finding a peer group. " [1]
>
> —Howard Rheingold, *The Virtual Community*, 1994

Player avatars in first-person shooting games, such as the popular Halo series, are often powerful warriors with futuristic weapons and armor.

> " Online it doesn't matter what you look like. Virtual worlds bring people together— everyone is on common ground. In the real world, people can be uncomfortable around me before they get to know me and realize that, apart from my outer appearance, I'm just like them. "[3]
>
> —Jason Rowe, young man with significant physical disabilities, 2013

by his disease. For Rowe, "The computer screen is my window to the world."[2]

WHAT YOUR AVATAR IS REALLY SAYING

While some people may design avatars that are mostly accurate representations of their real-world selves, and others may choose ones that are their opposites, researchers have found that no matter the avatar, it says

something about one's real-world personality. In a study published in 2015, psychology PhD student Katrina Fong found, "Who we are in real life does to some extent drive our choices in deciding how to represent ourselves online."[4]

One of the traits she studied, for example, was agreeableness. In the study, subjects were asked to take a personality test and subsequently to create an avatar. Then, a different group of people was asked to rate the avatars on agreeableness. These people were able to accurately identify the personalities of the avatars' creators. This is in part because people can pick up on subtle clues about another's personality in both the real world and the virtual one.

WANT TO BE FRIENDS?

Katrina Fong's research shows making friends in the virtual world is not all that different from making friends in the real one. In her study of avatars, people were asked if they were interested in becoming online friends with others based on their avatars. The avatars that were most often chosen as potential friends were those with open eyes, a smile, and an oval-shaped face. In the real world, such features are attractive and suggest the person is more friendly and thus a better potential friend. Similarly, people were not interested in either virtual or real people who had a neutral expression.

Some online avatars are simplified, cartoony figures that users can customize to show off their personalities.

HISTORY OF GAMING

The first simple computer games made their debut in the 1950s. Computerized games continued to evolve through the years, becoming more interactive. Then, in 1971, the first coin-operated arcade-style game, *Computer Space*, debuted. While the game never became a cultural icon, it laid the foundation for arcade games that followed. The first in-home game was introduced in 1972. Soon companies introduced consoles that could play multiple games. The 1980s and 1990s saw further advances, with companies such as Atari, Nintendo, and Sega creating increasingly sophisticated games. By the year 2000, gamers could interact in fully 3-D worlds. And by 2016, computing power had improved enough to make realistic virtual-reality worlds possible. As the games became more sophisticated, gaming culture grew. Eventually, online communities of gamers emerged and interacted with other players around the world.

AVATARS AND THE REAL WORLD

Researchers have also discovered a correlation between people's chosen avatars and their satisfaction with their real-world lives. People who create avatars that are similar to their real identities, both physically and in personality, tend to be those who are most satisfied with their lives. Similarly, those who are dissatisfied are more likely to game using avatars with qualities they wish they possessed themselves. Teens are also more likely to choose avatars different from their real-world identities. This is not necessarily due to dissatisfaction but may be because they are experimenting while trying to establish their own identities.

While individuals may be the creators of their avatars, the avatars themselves oftentimes end up influencing the individual. People who are naturally shy or introverted may choose avatars that are quite the opposite, giving them a safe space in which to test out different personality traits. For some, the opportunity to play a character that is bold and assertive in the virtual world enables them to build skills and confidence that carry over to the real world. This has been called the Proteus effect, after the Greek god Proteus, who had the ability to transform himself into other figures. A study at Stanford University's Virtual Human Interaction Lab discovered that people are, in fact, influenced by their online identities, whether they are social media personas or avatars. The research found that not only do people tend to take on qualities of their personas as they move about the virtual world, but the effects extend into their real world as well. In the lab, for example, people who were assigned superhero avatars for the study were found to be more willing to help people in the real world afterward.

All of the discussion and research about online identity and avatars suggests that perhaps one's online identity is not a second self but is rather

AVATARS IN E-COMMERCE

Businesses have online identities as much as individuals do, and they spend a good deal of time and money on those identities. Part of that marketing strategy includes creating avatars to represent the company and help with customer service on their websites. Clifford Nass, a professor of communication at Stanford University, believes an avatar needs to be able to establish a connection with customers and to be as similar as possible to the average customer in terms of posture, appearance, voice, and language. By creating an online persona customers can relate to and interact with, the company creates trust, which it hopes will translate to purchases.

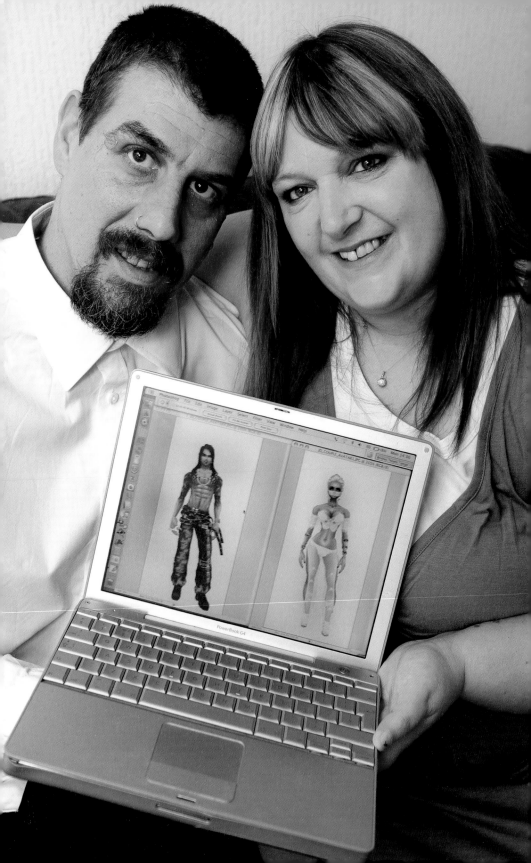

an extension of one's real-world self. Moreover, while some may warn that gaming is undermining community in the real world, people who are a part of the virtual gaming world claim quite the opposite. In online, interactive communities, people are able to interact, hang out, connect, collaborate, create, lead, and share experiences. Further, these shared spaces have expectations and a culture all their own. For many, this type of environment is empowering in both the virtual world and the real one.

In 2012, British couple Marie and Jay Coulbeck married in real life after their avatars met online.

THE GAMES OF THE NSA

Both US and British spies participate in massively multiplayer online role-playing games such as *World of Warcraft* and *Second Life* as a means to collect data and conduct surveillance. The National Security Agency (NSA), which operates under the US Department of Defense, believed terrorists or criminals could use online games to plan attacks, move money, or communicate secretly. Intelligence officials were concerned chat features in games would allow people to use fake names and avatars to exchange information. Intelligence agencies had so many spies lurking in the virtual world that the agencies were concerned their avatars might accidentally meet one another.

Despite the efforts by the NSA, there have been no significant counterterrorism victories as a result of the games. Some believe the government's efforts were misguided. Gamers were upset the games were being used for intelligence surveillance and data collection, and they were also left wondering whether the avatars they met were spies or just other gamers.

Second Life was launched in 2003 and was still active by 2016.

CHAPTER 7

CYBERCRIME

In the virtual world, personal information can be bought, sold, and traded with ease, making it possible for criminals to steal identities. According to the Federal Bureau of Investigation (FBI), identity theft happens "when someone unlawfully obtains another's personal information and uses it to commit theft or fraud."[1] Because so much of an individual's information is online in the digital age, thieves are able to take advantage. They do so by acquiring social security numbers, birth dates, addresses, phone numbers, financial account information, credit card information, and passwords. Once they have the information, they can use it to create a new identity or gain access to an individual's money.

Another way criminals access someone's personal information is by phishing or pharming. In the case of phishing, a scammer sends out e-mails that appear to be from a trustworthy institution but in fact are an attempt to trick someone into giving out personal information. Pharming is similar, but instead of tricking an online user through a fake e-mail or link, pharming automatically redirects individuals to a fake website where individual information is stolen.

An FBI agent gives a presentation to the National Cyber-Forensics & Training Alliance, a collaboration between universities, the government, and corporations focusing on cybercrime.

CYBERSECURITY EXECUTIVE ORDERS

During President Obama's two terms in office, he recognized the potential dangers of cybercrimes to US security and economics and realized the nation was not adequately prepared to deal with these threats. Accordingly, he made cybersecurity a priority and signed several executive orders to address the issue. One, Improving Critical Infrastructure Cybersecurity, was signed in February 2013. The order calls for improved information sharing between the government and private businesses, as well as a collaborative effort between the two to develop standards for protecting critical infrastructure.

A 2014 order, Improving the Security of Consumer Financial Transactions, was signed to help protect consumers from identity theft by improving credit card features, including adding a secure microchip to cards. Consumers would also be required to enter an identification number.

Obama signed another executive order, Blocking the Property of Certain Persons Engaging in Significant Malicious Cyber-Enabled Activities, in 2015. This order is a framework to expand and improve information sharing between private companies, and between companies and the government, to quickly and efficiently identify cyberthreats.

Adults are not the only ones at risk. Experts are seeing a growing trend in the theft of children's identities, thanks to the Internet and the amount of time kids spend online. In the past, child identity theft was generally limited to relatives of the child who had access to personal information, such as Social Security numbers. Nowadays, with kids online for hours every day, they have become easy targets for cybercriminals. Not only are children more likely to overshare online, they also respond to phishing or pharming scams. Once a criminal gets personal information,

President Obama held a cybersecurity discussion with business leaders at Stanford University in February 2015.

NATIONAL CYBER SECURITY AWARENESS MONTH

In an effort to make the security of cyberspace the shared responsibility of the virtual community, in 2004 the Department of Homeland Security declared October National Cyber Security Awareness Month. The department sought to make people aware of online crime, including data breaches, the use of malware to remotely control others' computers, fraud, identity theft, buying and selling illegal goods, the use of the internet by predators, and more. For its part, the government has created task forces to investigate these cyberthreats. For those who suspect or have witnessed cybercrimes, there is the Internet Crime Complaint Center, which fields online submissions in an effort to catch criminal activity. Through awareness efforts, the FBI hopes to educate the public about evolving cyberthreats and promote ethical cybercitizenship.

he or she can use it to steal money or take out loans. Families have had their children receive credit card offers and telemarking calls, both signs their child's identity had been compromised. For thieves, children make excellent targets because the identity theft may go unnoticed for years.

With this growth of child identity theft online, children are being warned not to accept friend invitations from unknown people. Likewise, experts caution kids to keep private information secret, to set up strong passwords that are never shared, and to turn on privacy settings on social networking sites.

FAKE IDENTITIES

While some people use the Internet to steal identities, others use it to create fake ones, as seen in the Manti Te'o catfishing scandal. A sock

As kids spend more time on the Internet, they may become more vulnerable to online identity theft.

puppet is another type of fake identity. It is an online identity created for the purposes of deception. The deception might be as simple as someone using an identity in order to be taken seriously or to promote certain ideas or beliefs, or even for profit or attention. One case involved a teenager named Kaycee Nicole who used her blog as a sort of diary about her battle with leukemia. Beginning in 1999, her story attracted many followers

> The Internet has become a battlefield for virtual personalities—all attempting to gather information to help their causes and hurt their enemies. [2]
>
> —Charles Seife, author, 2014

and sympathizers throughout her ups and downs. When she was said to have died in May 2001, the online community expressed its grief. And then one online user posted a question: "Is it possible that Kaycee did not exist?"[3] Eventually the story unraveled, revealing that Kaycee was, in fact, fictitious and was the creation of a woman seeking attention.

Other sock puppets are created to appear completely separate from their creators, and they are used to show support for the creator, give positive online reviews, criticize enemies, or engage in online feuds. The police also use sock puppets to stop crime. Officers purposely create fake online identities that appear unconnected to their departments in order to hang out on social media sites looking for criminal activity.

Law enforcement officers sometimes go undercover online, joining chat rooms to lure people, including child predators, into situations in which they can be arrested.

TAKING ILLEGAL ACTIVITY ONLINE: THE SILK ROAD

The Silk Road was a virtual marketplace where users could anonymously buy and sell illegal drugs, goods, and services. Between 2011 and 2013, the site's owners successfully evaded law enforcement, allowing criminals to operate beyond the reach of the law. According to the FBI, during the Silk Road's almost two years of operation, it "was used by thousands of drug dealers and other unlawful vendors to distribute hundreds of kilograms of illegal drugs and other unlawful goods and services to more than 100,000 buyers, and to launder hundreds of millions of dollars deriving from these unlawful transactions."[4] In addition to drug sales, other services included hacking services, malware sales, pirated media transactions, and forgery services for driver's licenses, Social Security numbers, passports, and credit cards.

The owner and operator of the website, Ross Ulbricht, created it solely for illegal purposes and to assure the anonymity of its users worldwide. He employed programmers and online administrators to keep the service operating. Overall, the FBI believes he generated more than $13 million in sales.[5] Once the

A courtroom sketch produced in May 2015 shows Ulbricht awaiting sentencing.

site was shut down in October 2013, the authorities caught and charged Ulbricht. After his four-week federal trial in 2015, Ulbricht was found guilty on seven charges, including distributing narcotics through the Internet and conspiring to commit money laundering. He was sentenced to life in prison on May 29, 2015.

The family of Alex Boston, 14, filed a lawsuit against classmates who set up fake social media pages to harass and bully her.

TROLLING AND CYBERBULLYING

The anonymity of the Internet has also led to an increase in trolling, the posting of intentionally offensive, rude, or aggressive messages to stir up arguments online. Cyberbullying has become a national problem as well. While bullying itself is not new, the Internet can make it much more severe. No longer are schoolyard feuds and hallway rumors left behind after the last bell. In the virtual world, victims can be bullied 24 hours a day, seven days a week. They are no longer safe even at home. Moreover, the online platform gives their humiliation an extremely public audience, and online posts never completely go away.

According to statistics from the Cyberbully Research Center, more than 30 percent of kids have experienced some kind of online harassment.[6] This can include having rumors posted about them online, receiving mean or hurtful comments, getting threats of physical harm, or having mean or hurtful photos of them posted. Increasingly, news headlines are revealing the real-world implications of this cyberbullying. The 2006 story of 13-year-old Megan Meier

HISTORY OF SOCK PUPPETRY

The act of creating a false identity in order to promote or denounce someone or something is not a digital-age invention. Sock puppetry was used by Sir Isaac Newton. Newton, a pioneering physicist, was one of two people who independently developed calculus in the 1600s. Gottfried Leibniz actually published his ideas first, but a dispute ensued and the two men wanted a scientific authority to settle it. The Royal Society of London, under the control of Newton himself, was selected for this task. The case was naturally settled in his favor. Afterward, the journal *Philosophical Transactions* published a review supporting the decision. Newton was later found to have been the author of this review.

received national attention. Megan made a friend named Josh on the social networking site MySpace. She exchanged regular messages with him at the beginning of her eighth grade year under the watchful eye of her parents. For the first time, she had a boy interested in her, and she was thrilled by the attention. Then in October, Megan unexpectedly got a message from Josh saying he had heard she was mean and he was not sure he wanted to be friends anymore. Josh had also apparently shared her posts with others, and Megan received an onslaught of hateful messages. The last message read, "The world would be a better place without you."[7] Megan hung herself in her room, and she died the next day. The police investigation uncovered the truth—Josh had never existed. Another family had created the fictitious account to monitor what Megan said about their own daughter. Megan's family started the Megan Meier Foundation in an effort to change the laws about cyberbullying, making it a crime. Unfortunately, as of 2015, most states did not include cyberbullying in their antibullying laws.

After her daughter's suicide, Megan's mother, Christina, traveled around the country talking to students about bullying.

CHAPTER 8

PRIVACY AND ANONYMITY

Whether to use real names or pseudonyms has become a great debate in the virtual world. Some believe anonymity online is a good thing, and that it should be a right of people online, especially at a time of growing privacy concerns. Yet those interested in trolling, catfishing, and cybercrimes also value anonymity.

A CASE FOR ANONYMITY

Some Internet users simply prefer anonymity. In the virtual world, they create a "brand," and that is how others know them as they blog, review, tweet, and post in different forums. For many, this branding is a way to carefully construct an online identity and a reputation that may differ from their real-world self. What matters, some believe, is not the real-world self, but the self that is created online through these interactions. While people may not know each other in the traditional, real-world sense, online users get to know each other and become friends in the virtual world based on online identities. Just as one leaves an impression when meeting others in person, so too do users when they

Anonymity is key to the online activism group known as Anonymous. Its members wear masks during public demonstrations to maintain anonymity.

COMPLETE ANONYMITY

Anonymity is heavily emphasized on the website 4chan. In 2003, 15-year-old Christopher Poole created a forum for his friends to use. Since then, the site has expanded to include dozens of different message boards on different topics. It sees hundreds of thousands of posts a day. This may not sound all that different from other social media platforms. A key difference is that it is completely anonymous, no registration is required to post, and there are no archives on the site. Poole believes this complete anonymity leads to raw and unfiltered content. Others argue that anonymity is dangerous, allowing people to say anything in a place where all rules are gone. While Poole recognizes there are risks, he believes the positives are empowering and valuable, especially in light of the push for real names online.

meet in virtual communities. In these communities, reputation matters.

Christopher Poole, founder of anonymous message board 4chan, is critical of the growing number of "real name" policies online, saying they keep people from freely exploring the many sides of themselves. Instead, he believes anonymity empowers people to safely and easily present their many sides in the virtual world. He and others believe anonymity is critical to being able to freely express oneself, to seek information or ask questions, or to be a part of groups a person might not feel comfortable with in the real world. This is especially true for activists, those participating in online health forums, and those exploring sexual orientation. Others want to participate

Christopher Poole speaks at a tech conference in 2011.

online anonymously for political reasons, worrying that speaking out against authority may get them in serious trouble or put them in danger.

Anonymity, for example, fueled the Arab Spring uprisings in 2011, which toppled governments in several Middle Eastern and North African countries. In many of these nations, personal expression and free speech are restricted. Social media gave individuals a platform on which they could mobilize for demonstrations and gatherings.

A study from the University of Washington analyzed massive amounts of social media content in the aftermath of the revolutions. Project leader Philip Howard said, "Our evidence suggests that social media carried a cascade of messages about freedom and democracy across North Africa and the Middle East, and helped raise expectations for the success of political uprising. People who shared interest in democracy built extensive social networks and organized political action. Social media became a critical part of the toolkit for greater freedom."[1] Activists, shielded by anonymity, could communicate, mobilize, and participate in the revolutions. They could also inform the rest of the world about what was going on in these countries. The actual protests occurred on real-world streets, but the anonymity of the virtual world was the catalyst for change.

Anonymity in the virtual world can also empower users to break free of the restrictions of the real world. The goal can be as simple as wanting to present a different physical image to escape

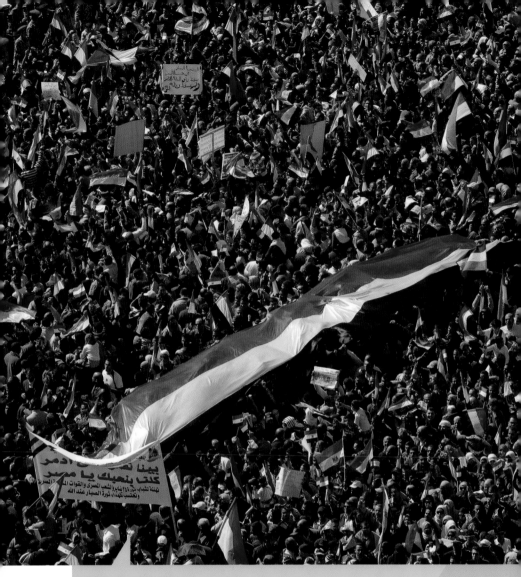

Many Arab Spring uprisings, including the revolution in Egypt, were organized with the help of social media tools.

physical limitations, to avoid real-world preconceptions based on race, gender, and age, or to present a personality that is more outgoing and confident. For those who have past criminal records or those who have been victims, an anonymous profile gives them a clean slate where they can rebuild their identity.

CHILDREN'S ONLINE PRIVACY PROTECTION ACT

As early as 1998, the US government recognized the need to protect children's identities online, resulting in the passage of the Children's Online Privacy Protection Act (COPPA). The act gives parents a measure of control over the personal information that can be collected from children under the age of 13 as they explore the virtual world. If a site requests personal information, the business must contact parents or legal guardians directly. They need to seek permission to collect data such as names, phone numbers, locations, and photos. If a site or app requests these kinds of information, parents should get a message about how their child's information will be collected and used, along with a request for parental consent. Since the act's initial passage, the Internet has grown in ways lawmakers did not anticipate. The explosion of social media has changed the way personal information is shared online. As a result, the act was updated in 2013 with new provisions, including expanded definitions to include new technologies and new types of information, such as real-world locations determined by the global positioning system (GPS).

The debate about anonymity heats up, however, when considering increases in cyberbullying, identity theft, fraud, and sock puppetry. Anonymity keeps the individuals who perpetrate these activities from being held accountable. Many people say and do things they may not otherwise do in real-world interactions, a phenomenon known as the online disinhibition effect. This happens because in the virtual world people often feel not only invisible but also disconnected from their real-world selves. They may become disassociated from the real world and feel there are no authority figures present.

> In the real world people subconsciously monitor the behaviour of others around them and adapt their own behaviour accordingly. . . . Online we do not have such feedback mechanisms.[2]
>
> —Graham Jones, Internet psychologist, 2013

For some this means merely the opportunity to freely express themselves. For others, anonymity represents permission to be more aggressive and cruel. This can lead to cyberbullying.

PRIVACY MATTERS, TOO

Despite the disinhibitions anonymity affords, privacy is nonetheless valuable. In the real world, people can choose when and where to have private conversations. They can determine the audience that hears them. Discussions about one's health, for example, are usually with a doctor, or perhaps close friends and family. Conversely, in the virtual world without anonymity, almost nothing is private. The same person having real-world conversations about health problems may also want to participate in an online health forum, visit different websites for more information, or buy a book on the subject online. Yet if these people use their real names, their private concerns

PRIVACY AND HEALTH

In the real world, an individual's health information is protected by law. Health-care professionals and medical facilities may collect patients' data, but how that data is used and shared is restricted. In this way, it is kept private. But if one chooses to share medical information in the virtual world, this privacy is not maintained. Those who engage in conversations about their health on social media, fill out health quizzes, or share genetic information to trace ancestry cannot expect any privacy. In fact, information shared online can potentially become accessible to anyone. The information could be read not only by family and friends, but also by a larger peer group, prospective employers, college admissions offices, and businesses collecting data for targeted advertising.

REPUTATION MANAGEMENT

For those who are concerned that their online reputations may be somewhat tarnished, there are services that can help. Online reputation management companies help individuals create an online identity makeover to remove embarrassing photos, eliminate poor work histories, and generally take back control over what others can find out about them online.

gain a public audience. People using their real names cannot expect privacy without greatly censoring what they say and how they interact with others.

Personal lives aside, the way businesses collect and use data about individuals can leave Internet users feeling as though they are losing control of their own information. Online users regularly see the effects of this data collection in the form of targeted advertising based on their past online purchases, browsing, and interactions. As a result, a growing number of online services have sprung up that help individuals remove data from their online profiles so businesses and other users cannot view it.

Anonymity and privacy are important aspects of online identity. They offer a way to gain more control over the persona one presents in different contexts and in front of different audiences. Despite the advantages of anonymity and the value of privacy, there is nonetheless a push for people to use their real names online.

Facebook's Mark Zuckerberg speaks to advertisers in 2007 about his social network's potential as an advertising platform.

CHAPTER 9

IDENTITY IN THE DIGITAL AGE

The growing movement toward using real names for online identities has escalated into heated debates over the use of real names versus pseudonyms. One of the largest social media sites, Facebook, has a real-name policy because, according to former company spokesperson Randi Zuckerberg, "People behave a lot better when they have their real names down."[1]

FACEBOOK'S REAL NAME POLICY

Facebook's real name policy requires users to use the name friends and family know them by. It is an effort to protect users against trolling, bullying, scams, hate speech, and other bad virtual world behavior. "Our ability to successfully protect against [that] with this policy has borne out the reality that this policy, on balance, and when applied carefully, is a very powerful force for good," the company claims.[2] To enforce the policy, Facebook flags names suspected of being faked and suspends accounts. Users must then provide some kind of identification as proof of their names.

Despite opposition, Facebook's cofounder Mark Zuckerberg vehemently defended the policy, stating, "Having two identities

Randi Zuckerberg worked at Facebook until 2011.

for yourself is an example of a lack of integrity."[3] The opposition, however, continued arguing individuals in vulnerable or marginalized groups in society were either silenced or put in danger by Facebook's real name policy. These groups included ethnic minorities, political dissidents, activists, the LGBTQ community, and abuse victims.

As a result, various rights groups protested Facebook's policy. In October 2015, the Nameless Coalition, a group of civil rights organizations and individuals against the real name policy, presented Facebook with a letter asking for changes. Under the weight of intense pressure, Facebook finally announced adjustments to its real name policy in December 2015. It added tools that allow individuals to share special circumstances that dictate the use of a name other than their real one. In addition, those reporting the use of fake names are required to provide context for their complaint.

MAJORITY ILLUSION

Social networks enable people to connect and create communities. But many Internet users are not aware of how these networks can shape, bias, or skew their social perceptions. Sometimes the networks may make it seem as though a majority of people believe a particular thing. This is called the majority illusion. A person's social perceptions—what one believes to be true, fashionable, trendy, or common—are largely affected by who one connects with. People know only what is going on in their part of the network, which in reality is only a tiny sliver of the overall population. They make false assumptions based on their friends' behaviors instead of knowledge of society as a whole.

People from a wide variety of groups opposed Facebook's real name policy.

As of 2016, more than three billion people had connected to the Internet. These people posted, tweeted, e-mailed, linked, surfed, bought, researched, read, and participated in the virtual world. Perhaps the only thing they all have in common is that, at some point, they will die. There are now services that let users decide before they die what will happen to their digital archives and personal accounts. Users can also create a message that can be posted to Facebook after they die. Some experts believe computers will eventually be able to analyze one's lifetime of Internet activity to the extent that the online identity will be able to continue interacting with fellow users after one's real-world death.

While Facebook believes asking individuals to share their special circumstances will enable the company to understand unique situations, others believe asking vulnerable individuals to share even more information about their circumstances is both risky and misguided.

PROTECTING ONE'S IDENTITY

What is also at risk for many online users is the line between public and private identities. Mobile technology has made it especially easy for people to stay connected to their public personas even at home or at traditionally private times. More and more people, for example, bring work home with them or even on vacation. And conversely, time with friends used to be limited during the school day to passing periods, lunch, and after school, but now students can stay connected to their friends constantly, bringing their private lives into public. Further, with private thoughts, images, and interactions increasingly out in the open, it is more important

Facebook's real name requirement has frustrated some groups that place a high priority on anonymity or unconventional names.

than ever to consider how to manage private information and personas.

No matter whether a person uses a real name or a pseudonym, publically or privately, managing and protecting one's online identity is essential. Identities online leave footprints, building a reputation with each post and interaction. One rule of thumb some people use online is that they should not post anything they would not want their grandmother to see. This helps them ensure they are putting their best representation into the public eye. Some people manage their identities simply by being careful about choosing which communities they belong to, political affiliations they declare, and photos they post.

Experts recommend avoiding sharing information such as social security numbers, birth dates, and addresses, except with reputable sites. They say passwords should be strong, changed regularly, and never shared with others. Users should pick different passwords for different sites, and privacy settings should be activated on social media and mobile phones.

People take these kinds of precautions because their identities are at stake. How the

> " It's one of the great paradoxes of our time that the very technologies that empower us to do great good can also be used to undermine us and inflict great harm. "[4]
>
> —President Barack Obama, February 13, 2015

Paying close attention to how your online identity is being constructed is critical in the information age.

Internet will continue evolving and expanding in the coming decades is anyone's guess. What is certain is that it will continue to grow and become even more closely tied to everyday life. Online communities are likely to remain an integral part of the digital age. Online identities provide people with the ability to participate, connect, create, interact, and explore like never before.

The Internet and social networking services have forever changed the role of identity in modern culture.

ESSENTIAL FACTS

MAJOR EVENTS

» On October 21, 1998, the Children's Online Privacy Protection Act (COPPA) passed. It was designed to help protect the privacy and identity of children as they use the Internet.

» In 2004, Mark Zuckerberg launched Facebook, one of the world's largest social networking sites.

» In 2011, social media and online anonymity helped make the Arab Spring possible.

» In 2012, the Manti Te'o catfishing story made national headlines.

KEY PLAYERS

» President Barack Obama was the first US president to have an online presence and to leverage social media to his benefit.

» Douglas Rushkoff is a digital media critic and professor of media theory and digital economics at CUNY/Queens. He explores media, technology, and culture.

» Sherry Turkle is a professor of the social studies of science and technology at the Massachusetts Institute of Technology. She investigates humans' relationships with each other and with technology in the digital age.

» Mark Zuckerberg is the cofounder of Facebook, which has transformed social media and the role it plays in people's real-world and online identities.

IMPACT ON SOCIETY

In many ways, one's online identity is like a second self, though some contend it is merely an extension of one's real-world self. Online communications and interactions are reshaping relationships and communities; they have become an integral part of how people in the early 2000s socialize. An online identity allows individuals to freely roam the virtual world at all hours of the day or night, free from many of the prejudices and limitations they might find in the physical world. People can explore their identities, pursue varied interests, and create social networks. Online identities have given individuals an unprecedented level of freedom to participate, connect, create, interact, and explore as never before.

QUOTE

"The computer screen is my window to the world."

—*Jason Rowe, physically disabled Internet user*

GLOSSARY

AVATAR

A character or icon that represents someone online.

CATFISHING

Creating a false identity online in order to trick someone else, oftentimes to lure someone into a relationship.

CRITICAL INFRASTRUCTURE

Physical and virtual resources so vital to the United States that the incapacity or destruction of such resources would negatively affect security, the economy, or public health or safety.

CYBERBULLYING

The use of the Internet to bully or harass, including sending intimidating messages, posting unwanted photos and videos, or creating false profiles.

CYBERSPACE

The online world of the Internet and computer networks.

DIGIPHRENIA

How technology allows people to be in more than one place, and to be more than one self, at the same time.

DISINHIBITION

A lack of personal restraint with respect to one's actions.

EMPATHY

Being able to understand and share another person's thoughts and feelings.

IDENTITY THEFT

The use of another's personal information to commit theft or fraud.

PERSONA

The image or personality that one presents to the world through actions, speech, and appearance.

PHARMING

Tricking online users through a fake email or link to redirect them to a fake website in order to steal personal information.

PHISHING

An Internet scam used by thieves to steal information and money from victims, or to install malicious software.

SOCK PUPPETRY

The use of a false online identity for the purposes of deception.

TROLLING

Posting cruel or offensive content online with the intent of making someone angry or upset.

ADDITIONAL RESOURCES

SELECTED BIBLIOGRAPHY

Boyd, Danah. *It's Complicated: The Social Lives of Networked Teens*. New Haven, CT: Yale UP, 2014. Print.

Claypoole, Ted, and Theresa Payton. *Protecting Your Internet Identity*. Lanham, MD: Rowman & Littlefield, 2012. Print.

Generation Like. Frank Koughan and Douglas Rushkoff, producers. PBS Frontline. PBS, 18 Feb. 2014. Web. 23 Nov. 2015.

Harris, Frances Jacobson. *I Found It on the Internet*. Chicago, IL: American Library Association, 2011. Print.

FURTHER READINGS

Eboch, M. M. *Big Data and Privacy Rights*. Minneapolis, MN: Abdo, 2016. Print.

Patchin, Justin W., and Sameer Hinduja. *Words Wound: Delete Cyberbullying and Make Kindness Go Viral*. Minneapolis, MN: Free Spirit, 2014. Print.

WEBSITES

To learn more about Essential Library of the Information Age, visit **booklinks.abdopublishing.com**. These links are routinely monitored and updated to provide the most current information available.

FOR MORE INFORMATION

For more information on this subject, contact or visit the following organizations:

DoSomething.org

19 West Twenty-First Street, Eighth Floor
New York, NY 10010
http://www.dosomething.org

This organization helps young people connect, communicate, and mobilize online in order to create social change in the real world.

Federal Bureau of Investigation (FBI)

935 Pennsylvania Avenue Northwest
Washington, DC 20535
202-324-3000
https://www.fbi.gov

The FBI protects and defends the United States and its citizens, which includes a focus on cybersecurity to mitigate and guard against cyberthreats.

SOURCE NOTES

CHAPTER 1. IDENTITY

1. Paul Myerberg. "A Timeline of the Manti Te'o Girlfriend Hoax Story." *ESPN*. ESPN, 18 Jan. 2013. Web. 2 Nov. 2015.

2. Angela Thomas. *Youth Online— Identity and Literacy in the Digital Age*. New York: Peter Lang, 2007. Print. 5.

CHAPTER 2. IDENTITY AND SOCIAL INTERACTION

1. Matt Ivester. *lol…OMG!* Reno, NV: Serra Knight, 2012. Print. 13.

2. Kyle Chayka. "Do You Own Your Identity Online?" *Pacific Standard*. Miller-McCune Center for Research, 4 Apr. 2014. Web. 23 Nov. 2015.

3. Ted Claypoole and Theresa Payton. *Protecting Your Internet Identity*. Lanham, MD: Rowman & Littlefield, 2012. Print. 43.

CHAPTER 3. THE SECOND SELF

1. Aleks Krotoski. "Online Identity: Can We Really Be Whoever We Want To Be?" *Guardian*. Guardian News, 18 June 2011. Web. 15 Nov. 2015.

2. Ibid.

3. Reggie Ugwu. "The Unbreakable Rebecca Black." *BuzzFeed*. BuzzFeed, 6 Aug. 2015. Web. 24 Mar. 2016.

4. Kyle Chayka. "Do You Own Your Identity Online?" *Pacific Standard*. Miller-McCune Center for Research, 4 Apr. 2014. Web. 23 Nov. 2015.

CHAPTER 4. WHO IS LOOKING?

1. Douglas T. Kenrick. "Science and the Online Dating Profile." *Psychology Today*. Sussex, 17 Mar. 2015. Web. 29 Nov. 2015.

2. Jon Ronson. "How One Stupid Tweet Blew Up Justine Sacco's Life." *New York Times Magazine*. New York Times, 12 Feb. 2015. Web. 5 Feb. 2016.

3. Judith S. Donath. "We Need Online Alter Egos Now More Than Ever." *Wired*. Condé Nast, 25 Apr. 2014. Web. 25 Nov. 2015.

4. "Coca-Cola." *Twitter*. Twitter, 2016. Web. 24 Mar. 2016.

5. Kyle Chayka. "Do You Own Your Identity Online?" *Pacific Standard*. Miller-McCune Center for Research, 4 Apr. 2014. Web. 23 Nov. 2015.

CHAPTER 5. REDEFINING RELATIONSHIPS

1. "Sherry Turkle: Connected, But Alone?" *TED*. TED, Feb. 2012. Web. 23 Nov. 2015.

2. "Gangs Find New Home on the Internet." *PoliceOne*. PoliceOne.com, 12 Jan. 2014. Web. 28 Nov. 2015.

3. Danah Boyd. *It's Complicated—The Social Lives of Networked Teens*. New Haven, CT: Yale UP, 2014. Print. 84.

4. Nancy Lublin. "Slacktivism: Helping Humanity with the Click of a Mouse." *Fast Company*. Mansueto Ventures, 1 May 2010. Web. 29 Nov. 2015.

5. "Who We Are." *Do Something*. DoSomething.org, n.d. Web. 28 Nov. 2015.

6. Alexis Manrodt. "The New Face of Teen Activism." *Teen Vogue*. Condé Nast, 8 Apr. 2014. Web. 26 Nov. 2015.

7. Juliet Eilperin. "Here's How the First President of the Social Media Age Has Chosen to Connect with Americans." *Washington Post*. Washington Post, 26 May 2015. Web. 29 Nov. 2015.

8. "Engage and Connect." *White House*. White House, 2016. Web. 25 Mar. 2016.

9. Alexis Manrodt. "The New Face of Teen Activism." *Teen Vogue*. Condé Nast, 8 Apr. 2014. Web. 26 Nov. 2015.

SOURCE NOTES CONT.

CHAPTER 6. THE ALTER EGO IN ACTION

1. Keith Stuart. "Gamer Communities: The Positive Side." *Guardian*. Guardian News, 31 July 2013. Web. 28 Nov. 2015.

2. Karen Lowton. *Researching Later Life and Ageing: Expanding Qualitative Research Horizons*. Ed. Miranda Leontowitsch. New York: Palgrave Macmillan, 2012. Print. 52.

3. Ibid.

4. Alison Bruzek. "Your Online Avatar May Reveal More about You Than You'd Think." *NPR*. NPR, 13 Jan. 2015. Web. 28 Nov. 2015.

CHAPTER 7. CYBERCRIME

1. "Identity Theft Overview." *Federal Bureau of Investigation*. FBI, n.d. Web. 27 Nov. 2015.

2. Charles Seife. *Virtual Unreality*. New York: Viking, 2014. Print. 55.

3. Ibid. 50.

4. "Ross Ulbricht, aka Dread Pirate Roberts, Sentenced in Manhattan Federal Court to Life in Prison." *Federal Bureau of Investigation*. FBI, 29 May 2015. Web. 27 Nov. 2015.

5. Ibid.

6. "2015 Cyberbullying Data." *Cyberbullying Research Center.* Cyberbullying Research Center, 1 May 2015. Web. 27 Nov. 2015.

7. Steve Pokin. "Megan's Story." *Megan Meier Foundation.* Megan Meier Foundation, 13 Nov. 2007. Web. 21 Nov. 2015.

CHAPTER 8. PRIVACY AND ANONYMITY

1. Catherine O'Donnell. "New Study Quantifies Use of Social Media in Arab Spring." *UW Today.* University of Washington, 12 Sept. 2011. Web. 27 Nov. 2015.

2. Alan Martin. "Online Disinhibition and the Psychology of Trolling." *Wired.co.uk.* Condé Nast, 30 May 2013. Web. 27 Nov. 2015.

CHAPTER 9. IDENTITY IN THE DIGITAL AGE

1. Ki Mae Heussner. "The Internet Identity Crisis." *Adweek.* Adweek, 6 Feb. 2012. Web. 27 Nov. 2015.

2. David Lee. "Facebook Amends 'Real Name' Policy after Protests." *BBC News.* BBC, 15 Dec. 2015. Web. 6 Feb. 2016.

3. Ki Mae Heussner. "The Internet Identity Crisis." *Adweek.* Adweek, 6 Feb. 2012. Web. 27 Nov. 2015.

4. Katie Zezima. "Obama Signs Order to Protect Consumers from Identity Theft." *Washington Post.* Washington Post, 17 Oct. 2014. Web. 27 Nov. 2015.

INDEX

ABOUT THE AUTHOR

Laura Perdew is an author, writing consultant, and former middle school teacher. She writes fiction and nonfiction for children, including numerous titles for the education market. She is also the author of *Kids on the Move! Colorado*, a guide to traveling through Colorado with children. Laura lives and plays in Boulder, Colorado, with her husband and twin boys.